TOP TIPS

Be the Best at Maths

Rebecca Rissman

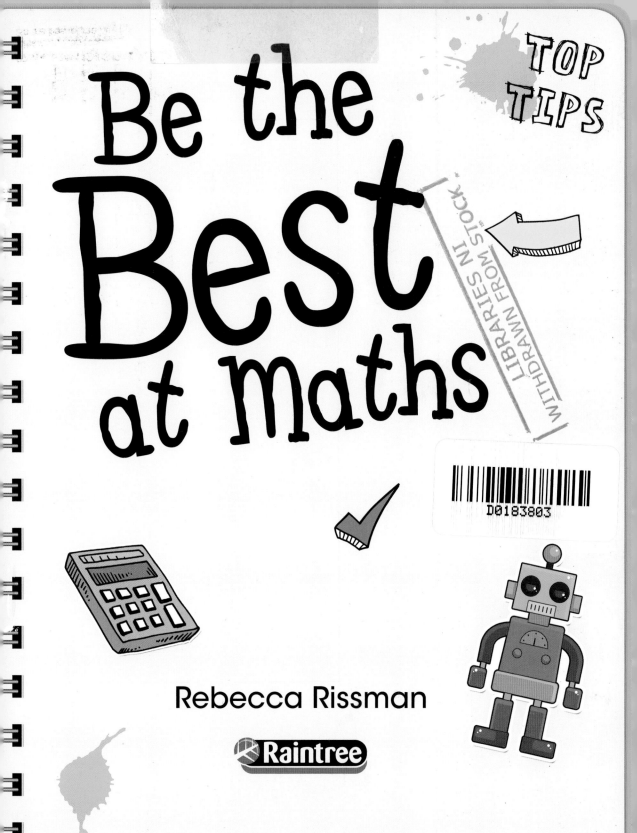

Raintree

www.raintreepublishers.co.uk
Visit our website to find out more information about Raintree books.

To order:

☎ Phone 0845 6044371

▤ Fax +44 (0) 1865 312263

✉ Email myorders@raintreepublishers.co.uk

Customers from outside the UK please telephone +44 1865 312262

Raintree is an imprint of Capstone Global Library Limited, a company incorporated in England and Wales having its registered office at 7 Pilgrim Street, London, EC4V 6LB – Registered company number: 6695582

Text © Capstone Global Library Limited 2013
First published in hardback in 2013
First published in paperback in 2014
The moral rights of the proprietor have been asserted.

Edited by Rebecca Rissman, Dan Nunn, and Adrian Vigliano
Designed by Joanna Hinton-Malivoire
Original illustrations © Capstone Global Library Ltd
Picture research by Ruth Blair
Production by Alison Parsons
Originated by Capstone Global Library
Printed in China by CTPS

ISBN 978 1 406 24106 8 (hardback)
16 15 14 13 12
10 9 8 7 6 5 4 3 2 1

ISBN 978 1 406 24111 2 (paperback)
17 16 15 14 13
10 9 8 7 6 5 4 3 2 1

British Library Cataloguing in Publication Data
A full catalogue record for this book is available from the British Library.

Acknowledgements
The author and publishers are grateful to the following for permission to reproduce copyright material: Shutterstock pp. 5 (© SergiyN), 6 (© Dmitry Naumov), 9 (© Alexander Cherednichenko), 10 (© gajluk), 12 (© Crystal Kirk), 15 (© indiwarm), 17 (© Chros), 18 (© PavelSvoboda), 21 (© Flashon Studio), 23 (© Philip Lange), 25 (© Nattika), 27 (© sergei telegin), 29 (© Lightfactor), 30 (© Lasse Kristensen). Background and design features reproduced with the permission of Shutterstock.

Cover photograph reproduced with the permission of Shutterstock and Shutterstock/© notkoo.

We would like to thank Nancy Harris for her invaluable help in the preparation of this book.

Every effort has been made to contact copyright holders of any material reproduced in this book. Any omissions will be rectified in subsequent printings if notice is given to the publisher.

Some words are shown in bold, **like this**. You can find out what they mean by looking in the glossary.

Contents

Get going!

People use maths every day. But sometimes maths can seem tricky. Don't worry! This book is full of helpful tips to make maths easier and more fun.

Top Tip

The more you use maths, the better you'll get. Start by trying to do 15 minutes of extra maths a day. Soon you'll be getting better and better!

Spot the symbol!

There are many signs, or **symbols**, in maths. Some symbols give you information. Numbers are symbols. They can tell you how many things there are.

I spy...

Other symbols tell you to do something:

+ add

– subtract

✖ multiply

÷ **divide**

Top Tip

Look over your maths problems for the symbols first!

Test that tip!

How many symbols can you spot in this problem?

$$5+3-4$$

These signs, or **symbols**, give you information about something:

 greater than

 less than

= equal to

Top Tip

Here's a great way to remember how to use the "greater than" and "less than" symbols. Imagine they are crocodiles' mouths. A crocodile will want to eat the bigger number. Its open mouth will always point that way.

Test that tip!

Which of these symbols goes between these numbers: <, >, or =?

9 ? 12

Line them up!

A **number line** is a great maths tool. You can use it to help you **add** or **subtract**. First you need to find the number you are adding or subtracting from. Then count the numerals away from it to find the answer!

0 1 2 3 4 5 6 7 8 9 10 11 12 13 14 15 16 17 18 19 20

12 add 4

Got it!

Test that tip!

Use a number line to solve this problem:

12+4=?

Top Tip

Remember that in addition problems, you can move the numbers to either side of the addition **symbol**.

15 + 4 = 4 + 15

This makes it easier to use the number line.

Use number bonds!

Sometimes you'll be asked to add a list of numbers together. It's easier to do this when you can group the numbers that add up to 10.

Look at this problem:
2 + 3 + 7 + 8 = ___. You can pull out the two pairs that add up to 10 (2 + 8 and 3 + 7). This makes it easier to come up with the sum of 20.

?

Test that tip!

$$9+4+1+6+3+7=?$$

Places everyone!

Remembering **place value** can make many maths problems easier to understand!

a one   a ten   a hundred

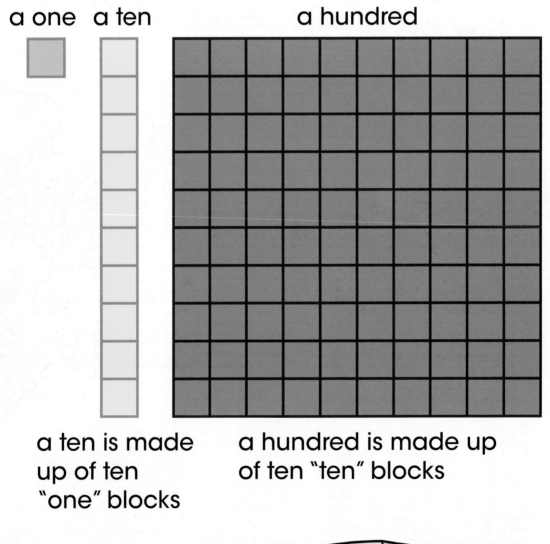

a ten is made up of ten "one" blocks

a hundred is made up of ten "ten" blocks

Top Tip

Break down large numbers into hundreds, tens, and ones. If you looked at the number 432, you would see:

4 hundreds

3 tens

2 ones

Now you're ready to use this in a maths problem!

Test that tip!

?

432-10=?

Punch it up!

Sometimes you will need to **round off** a number. You might round off to the nearest 5, 10, or 100. When rounding off to the nearest 10, look at the final numeral. If it is equal to or higher than 5, you will round it up. If it is lower than 5, you will round it down.

Top Tip

If you are unsure if you should round up or down to the nearest 10, use your fingers to count. If you have enough fingers to make a fist, it's time to punch it up, or round up!

POW!

Test that tip!

Should you round 54
up to 60 or down to 50?

Estimate it!

Sometimes you will have to **estimate**, or guess, how long something might take. One way to estimate is to use grouping!

How long?

Grouping numbers can help make big numbers easier to understand.

Test that tip!

How long will it take you to walk 400 steps?

1. Group the numbers: There are 4 groups of 100. How long would it take you to walk 100 steps?
2. Multiply your answer by 4!

?

Tricks by the number!

When you **multiply**, it can be helpful to remember some rules about different numbers.

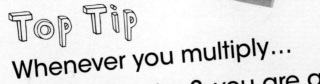

Top Tip

Whenever you multiply…

- a number by 2, you are adding that number to itself [9 x 2 = 9 + 9]
- a number by 5, the last digit of the answer will be either a 5 or a 0 [2 x 5 = 10, 3 x 5 = 15]
- an even number by 6, the answer will end in the same digit as the number you multiplied it by [6 x 2 = 12, 6 x 4 = 24]
- a number by 10, the answer will end in a zero [5 x 10 = 50]

Test that tip!

6x2=?

5x8=?

7x10=?

Use your hands!

When you multiply a number that's less than 10 by 9, you can use your hands to find the answer.

Top Tip

Stretch your hands out in front of you. Counting from left to right, put the finger down that represents the numeral you're multiplying by 9. The fingers to the left of your bent finger represent the first numeral in the answer. The fingers to the right represent the second numeral in the answer.

Test that tip!

9x5=?

23

Divide and conquer!

Here are some rules to remember that will make division a little easier!

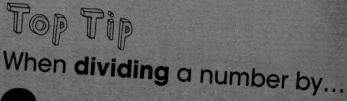

Top Tip

When **dividing** a number by...

2 cut it in half! But remember, you can only divide by 2 if a number is even.

4 just divide by 2... twice! $44 \div 4$ is the same as $44 \div 2 = 22$, and then $22 \div 2 = 11$.

Test that tip!

? 12÷2=?

24÷4=?

Not all division problems can give you a **whole number**. But here are some simple tricks to discover which will give you whole number answers.

Top Tip

When dividing a number by...

3 first add up all the digits until you get a single digit. If *that* number is divisible by 3, so is your original number!

32 ÷ 3 -> 3 + 2 = 5 -> 5 is not divisible by 3, so 32 is not divisible by 3

33 ÷ 3 -> 3 + 3 = 6 -> 6 is divisible by 3, so 33 will give you a whole number [33 ÷ 3 = 11]

6 if the number is divisible by *both* 2 and 3, it will be divisible by 6!

24 ÷ 2 = 12
24 ÷ 3 = 8
24 ÷ 6 = 4

Test that tip!

Is 43 divisible by 3?

Is 54 divisible by 6?

?

Study like a pro!

Set yourself up to succeed by practising these tips when you do your homework or study.

Top Tip

Before you start work, always:
➡ Eat a healthy snack
➡ Go somewhere quiet
➡ Make sure you have all the supplies you need:

- Textbook
- Scrap paper
- Calculator
- Timeline
- Pencils and rubber

Dream big!

Remember, learning maths can be useful in many ways as you grow up. You can use it in your job as an astronaut! You can use it when following a recipe for your favourite food. Studying maths is just the first step in a great adventure!

Ya-hoo!

Glossary

add to join two or more numbers together to make a new total

divide split into equal parts or groups

estimate close guess

multiply method for repeated addition

number line line with numbers written in numerical order. Number lines are good tools for learning addition and subtraction.

place value value of a digit's place in a number, such as ones, tens, or hundreds

round off bringing a number up or down to the nearest 5, 10, or 100

subtract to take away

symbol image or sign used in place of a word. For example, the symbol = stands for *equals*.

whole number number that has no fractional or decimal point. For example, 1, 2, and 3 are whole numbers, but 4 ½ is not.

Find out more

Books

Collins Revision: KS2 Maths (Collins, 2009)

Maths Made Easy: KS2 (series), Carol Vorderman (Dorling Kindersley, 2011)

Websites

www.bbc.co.uk/schools/ks2bitesize/maths
Visit the BBC Bitesize Maths website for help and advice with all your maths skills, plus interactive games, quizzes, and lots of other activities.

http://uk.ixl.com
On the IXL website you'll find a huge range of interactive quizzes and activities that will test and improve all your maths skills.

Index